DAGGER

IN

MEN'S

SMILES

LINUS AKALI I. SDV

Be wary of friends – they will betray you more quickly, for they are easily aroused to envy. They also become spoiled and tyrannical. But hire a former enemy and he will be more loyal than a friend, because he has more to prove. In fact you have more to fear from friends than from enemies. If you have no enemies, find a way to make them.

... Robert Greene

DEDICATION

In Memorial of my Beloved Parents, Late Mr. And Mrs Alphonsus Akali, who never smile to me with a hidden dagger.

ACKNOWLEDGEMENTS

To God be the glory. This work is God's doing and is very marvellous to my eyes. I owe God all the glory and honour for making this work a reality. I also wish to appreciate those who helped me in producing this work. I wish to acknowledge my religious congregation, the Vocationist Fathers and Brothers, for the opportunity given to me in this life. I acknowledge the advice and guidance of my family members, the Akalis for their love and cares. All my relatives and friends who showed me love and care, especially during my priestly ordination, I wish to appreciate you. I say thanks to you all.

This book could not have seen the light of the day without the efforts of Barrister Mrs Ngozi Obi, who painstakingly wrote the forward to this work. I say thanks to you for your kind heart. My regards to my beloved brother Chikodi Gerald who provided some useful ideas for this work, and also for typesetting this work. To all whom in one way or the other helped me to attain this status, may God reward you abundantly; His love shall never fail you all in Jesus name. To all who are victims of backbiting, prejudice, hatred, envy and jealousy, I pray the good Lord to plead your course. You shall be vindicated. To all my readers, I thank you and promise to keep up my ink for the betterment of our lives. God Bless you all! Linus Akali I. sdv (2016)

TABLE OF CONTENTS

MAN IN THE SOCIETY

LEADING STORY

It was only 7am and James was on his way to the village to see her ailing mum. It was a long journey since he took to travel by land, going from Lagos to Imo State. The vehicle he boarded moved a little bit late from the stipulated departure time. There was not the usual boom of passengers since it was not the season period. During seasonal period in Nigeria West Africa, passengers used to queue for tickets escalating the transport fare, but this time passengers are begged to buy tickets and the price consequently is low. But finally, the vehicle was able to depart for East. To travel from Lagos (western Nigeria) to the East of the country takes a long hours of journey because of the depleted state of the road. And because of the festive period, there are usually heavy traffics at certain cities along to eastern part.

James was ruminating with the content and the tune of the voice from the other end of the phone he answered the previous night that prompted the unplanned journey. He was starring at the green fresh shrubs along the road without paying any attention to them. The thought of the mind and perception are no near in consonance. The voice continued to re-echo, "Brother, there is trouble...mum...mum...mum". He had answered, "Yes, what happened...what happened to mum"? The voice continued echoing, "Please brother, Mum...please brother James come back!" It was his younger brother's voice and that night James knew something unusual has happened. His brother has not been that devastated before. He tried to call again to get the actual message but to no avail. James had to call his Uncle, Ugwunna, who told him to take the next flight if possible. He called off a scheduled meeting with certain customers in his small entrepreneur business and had to travel. The vehicle, ITC hummer bus, was speeding jin a very high velocity that what brought James to consciousness of his environment was some arguments between the driver and some furious passengers who were shouting at the speeding driver. Though this didn't calm his troubled heart, he was at least drawn to the theme of the argument.

"But what will be of him if the mum dies?" The dad died several years back leaving the poor widow to take the burden of raising their five kids with Jane, their house help. Thank God, they are all grownups now. But unfortunately, their mother has not has enjoyed the fruits of her labour. He was the only one who has started a small business; Mark and Jude are still jobless after their university studies. Mary and Joy, their elder sisters are also jobless, even praying for suitors. Jane, the house-help is quite ripped for marriage but has been suffering from one heart-break to another, but supposed to have her traditional wedding same day James received that phone-call. So what has actually happened?

The ITC bus arrived Owerri, the State capital at about 4pm amidst hold-ups and go-slows at various points along their way. But thank God the journey was safe. Though the slow vehicle movement continued in Owerri, James was able to reach his village in an hour's time. His mind was beating as fast as he approached the small track road leading to their compound. He was paying some silence attention and observing everyone that greeted him or passed him along the road. But he observe one thing, those who greeted him were mumbling the greetings; even his friends were not convincing in their greetings. Some women were pointing at him in a cajoling manner. "What must have happened?" he was querying his curious mind.

The entrance to his father's compound could have given him a sort of answer but that was not clear, as it seems someone has passed on. James was trying to hold his tears as groups of people were trooping out of their house. Still people were making some sort of comments that depicted a terrible omen. They were looking at him this time as they pass him instead of greeting him. A woman whispered to his hearing, "Bad son of a witch...like mother like son". James had his heart in his mouth. He ran into the house and saw his two sisters sitting beside his mother who was lying helplessly blind!

"What had happened?" he inquired. He was told the horrible story of his mother's hidden life. His mother, Ugboaku, had been envious of her house help who she has been training as her own daughter from infancy. Jane has grown up as a very pretty lady, though not much educated as she was not allowed to attain any higher institution, just because she was not her biological child. Mary and Joy, almost the same age with Jane had attended higher institution and were also very pretty ladies. But Jane has enviable character, which the other ladies lacked. This made her loved by people to the envy of Ugboaku. She pretended to love Jane equally as her other daughters. But who knows what a woman has in mind? Jane has had seven suitors but none succeeded in marrying her. It was when she went for prayers that it was revealed she was diabolically tied. Ugboaku has been after her using diabolical powers. But no one noticed this.

Jane went for deliverance, and was able to settle with a man. They fixed a traditional wedding on that faithful day, which Ugboaku was well aware of. Unknowing to all, she went to get a powder poison for mass destruction. On the wedding day, the woman was in charge of the stores were food and other edible items were kept. She went to carry out her evil plans, but unfortunately for her it boomeranged. As she was putting the poison in the food, there was a heavy blow of breeze that blew the powder into her eyes and she got instantly blind. She was panting and whiling to no avail. She wanted finish all the visitors coming for the wedding ceremony. Who would have thought that Ugboaku, who supposed to be the Mother of the day, is planning such an evil! No one could have expected that given her "supposedly" gestures of hospitality to all the invited. Appearance is sometimes deceptive, and care should be taken not to judge only by appearance, as human beings could be sometimes described as a "beautiful painted sepulchre; rotten inwardly while the outward is gorgeously painted.

FOREWORD

Generally speaking, one of the phenomena that have remained a problem in our contemporary society is the destruction of the sanctity of human lives. This is attributed to human intention and the radical change in our fundamental attitude towards life. Human intentions are so deceptive that an Igbo dictum illustrates it thus: "Iwe di n'obi, ochi di na eze" that is to say that one can be laughing but the mind is filled with hatred. A well known English dictum was illustrated by Bryan C.J. in an English medieval case when he held concerning intention that: "The devil himself knoweth not the intention of a man". This is correct because no one is capable of seeing into another's mind and of being able to state with absolute certainty what his intention is. Intention is not capable of positive proof; it can only be implied from overt acts.

Fr. Linus Akali in his treatment and analysis of the human intention cuts across the length and breadth of most areas of thought that readers of this book would not be left in doubt as regards the essential areas to browse for important information and ideas about the different ways of entrapping human persons bearing in mind that a person is more invulnerable to an attack of a friend than that of a known enemy.

The stories, quotes and prayers contained herein will be sources of encouragement, unity and solidarity for all that will read this book. There are lots of lessons to be learnt and if these lessons are put into practice, the fast eroding norms of our society will be restored to a reasonable extent.

Barr. Mrs. Ngozi Obi.

Ike Obeta and Co, Chamber

Nnewi, Anambra State.

INTRODUCTION

Dagger in men's smile is a Shakespearean thought. It means that wicked men smile neither out of kindness nor innocence of heart but hide their wicked intentions. It is also a way of saying they cannot be trusted. It suggests that behind someone's outward friendly attitude, there may be an ulterior motive. Thus let us begin by flashing back at where this thought originates – the Shakespearean play, Macbeth. In this little dialogue immediately after the murder of King Duncan was announced, involving Macbeth, Malcolm, Donalbain and some other soldiers around.

Macbeth: **Get this no fear to go! And when we have our frailties hid, that suffer in exposure, let us meet and question this most bloody piece of work.**
To know it further ,fears and scruples shake us .In the great hand of God i stand , and hence ,Against the un-divulged pretence i fight of treasonous malice.

Mac duff: And so do I.

All; so all

Macbeth: **let's briefly put on manly readiness and**

meet it the hall together.

All: well contented.

(Exeunt   all but Malcolm and   donalbain).

Malcolm: what will you do? Let's not consort with them. To show an unfelt sorrow is an office which the false man does easy. i' ll to England.

Donalbain: To Ireland, I, our separated fortune shall keep us both the safer where we are, there daggers in men's smiles. The near in blood, the nearer bloody.

Malcolm: This murderous shaft that shot hath not yet lighted   , and our safest way is to avoid the aim. Therefore   , to horse, and let us not be dainty of leave-taking, but shift away. There warrant   in   that theft steals itself when there no merely left.

Dagger in men smiles is a Shakespearean thought that shows that many times people pretends to be good before us while their hearts are evil. The story of Macbeth shows this particular conception. Macbeth was a cousin of king Duncan, the king of Scotland .He was a warrior and valour. He fought for the honour of the king. This story began with   Macbeth, a general in the army of King   Duncan, defeating the allied forces of Norway and Ireland, who were led by the traitor, Macdonald. Macbeth, the king's cousin is praised for his bravery and fighting prowess.

But when Macbeth and his friend Banquet were returning from the battle, they meet the three witches who have waited to greet them with prophecies. The made the prophecies, first to Macbeth, addressing him as "Thane of Glamis"."Thane of Cawdor" and the one to be king hereafter" Macbeth was stunned to silence. When banquo challenged them for his own prophecy, they told him that he will father a line of kings, though he himself will not be a king. While the two men were pondering   over the pronouncements, the witches vanished and another Thane came ,Ross, a messenger from the king who immediately fulfilled the prophecy by greeting Macbeth with the titles of "Thane of Cawdor "Macbeth being already Thane of Glamis.

When Macbeth   saw that the first prophecy is immediately fulfilled, he started harbouring the ambition to become a king. Reaching home, having written his wife about it, they started planning the evil .Duncan decided to stay at Macbeth castle at Inverness, Lady Macbeth started to hatch the plan of murdering him and to secure the throne for the husband, and Macbeth objected to this but was persuaded by his wife who challenged his manhood.

On that faithful night, Macbeth received the king with cheer and Joy, while his heart was already clutching on the dagger .The king was at peace, being at his Cousin's castle; the one who have helped him fight his enemy, without knowing what the heart has planned for him. In his face, Macbeth was a cheerful lover, of the king, but in his heart, he planned to "delete" him in order to have his prophecy fulfilled. No one can tell the heart from the facial appearance of individual.

That night, when the king was at sleep, Macbeth murdered him in cold blood. Having done the deed, he reunited with his wife. In accordance with her plan, Lady Macbeth frames Duncan's sleeping servants for the murder by placing the bloody dagger on them.

When in the morning Lennox and macduff, the loyal "Thane of fife" arrived, Macbeth led them to the king's chamber where they discovered Duncan corpse. In a feigned fit of anger, Macbeth murdered the guards before they   prove their innocence .Duncan sons flee Malcolm to England and Donalbain to Ireland recognizing that there is danger even when all around seemed to be fighting for their course.

Macbeth realizing that he will not be succeeds by his own children, since the witches had prophesied that Banquo's linage will be kings, planned to destroy Banquo and his family. He invited Banquo to a royal banquet with his only son Fleance, but planted two assassins to kill them. On the attempt, Banquo, his best friend was killed, but the son, Fleance escaped. Macbeth failed in attempt to un-turn the prophecy in his greediness.

This particular Shakespearean work has aroused

some reflections which, I believe, will be useful in our society today. People have been victimized by the ones they call their friends, those they loved and trusted. Many have been stabbed at the back by the ones they once favoured. Many have suffered the fate of the Shakespearean Julius Caesar. These daggers have never come in a dagger-form, less people will escape them. But they have always come in hidden cheers, praise songs and seeming good deeds. Many families have been destroyed because of wickedness of neighbours who envy their success or who want to use them as stepping stone to their own progressive ladder.

We are in a world which we ourselves have turned cruel. Though created to live at peace with one another having common goal, we often fight peace very far to reach. Man continues to be woe to man, in a fashion that dispel trust and desire to assist others. Many times, our society present to us an environment was good deeds are returned with evil, were trusted friends turning devil over night. The society we find ourselves now present to us seeming Love and unrealistic compassion, a situation where you cannot really differentiate a true friend from a faithful enemy. We are sometimes presented with enemies in friend's guise, people who laugh you to scone. Even in a large relations, one is always afraid of the group he belong to because of betrays and sabotage. Tell your friend the utmost secret of your heart, exposé yourself to a danger of death!

This little piece is geared to expose the cruelty we suffer from our fellow human beings who pretend to care for us and do us good but hiding their stabbing dagger. It is meant to warn us on our in guarded relationship, to sting us to consciousness of our society and help us know the better way to relate with others. This work stings us to consciousness of our individual difference and how to live with one another without arousing the feelings of Jealousy and envy. It helps us to deal with jealousy and envy when they eventually raise their ugly head in our midst. It traces the human acts of wickedness from the scriptural background and point to us the way of seeking God's mercy and guidance for a better life. This little master-piece will arouse some feeling and inspiration in you. You only have to browse the pages gradually, savouring each message with rational and logical conclusion. It is a must read for all who live and relate with others.

CHAPTER ONE

MAN IN THE SOCIETY

We human beings, according to the scripture are created in the image and likeness of God (Gen 1:28).Moulded from dust, were have the breath of life, which gives us the divine spark of life. God endowed us with great features, more than all created things. We are specially made with great intelligence and will. Human beings have a highly developed brain, capable of abstract reasoning, language and communication. We are gifted with the ability to solve our problems, to care for fellow human beings.

Also ,human beings are uniquely made, in the sense that we are opt mostly adept at utilizing systems of communication for self-expression, the exchange of ideas, and organization . Humans create complex social structures composed of many cooperating and competing group, from families to nation. God made us in the way that we not only live together in our kind, but also establish our social interaction with an extremely wide variety of values. These values give our relationship meaning and also help to define our life. To live together, we created some moral norms- "do" and "don'ts"- that help to model our lives.

As human beings also, we are noted for our desire to understand influence our environment. We are curious beings, seeking to know, explain and manipulate phenomena through science, philosophy. Mythology and religion .this natural curiosity has led us to the development of advanced tools and skills, which are passed down culturally, out of the whole creation, it is only human beings that developed the skills of building, making their cloths, cooking their food and many other things. God made him thus. Man can relate to developed himself and his endowments. This also defines us as social beings, and also jays why we need each other

He is a social being and lives in the society. His life revolves on how well he relates .society; on the other hand have a great role to play in our lives. But before we look at the role of the society to us, let us look at the meaning of a society.

A society or human society is a group of people related to each other through persistent relations, or a large social grouping, sharing the same geographical or virtual territory, subject to the same political authority and dominant cultural expectations. This human society is characterized by patterns of relationship that is different ways we relate with one another. This relation is between individuals who share a distinctive culture and institution; a given society may be described as the sum total of such relationships among its constituent members.

IN SEARCH OF ONE GOAL

A human society is naturally collaborative, in the sense that it's member through their co-operations, benefit in ways that would not otherwise be possible on an individual basic ,both individual and social benefits can thus be distinguished, or in many cases found to overlap. We are all in search of one goal – survival in life. This survival is a universal goal for all human persons. All our activities, our daily toils and our quest to succeed points to the desire to survive.

Thus there is commonness in a human society .People of the same goal who achieve their purpose through co-operation. This means that there is the need for solidarity in our quest to survive. Each person must contribute his own quota to see off failure. "United we stand, divided we fall" is an old maxim. We are one people made from one substance by one maker. Though we are like-minded people who are governed by their own norms and values within a dominant, large society, there is the need for collective efforts. There is the need for understanding and love. Our diversity only points to the extended view of society as an economic, social or industrial infrastructure, made up of varied collection of individuals.

The society also refers to an organized voluntary

association of people for religious, benevolent, cultural, scientific, political patriotic or other purpose. This points to the fact that we are created to live together for a purpose. The purpose of understanding and helping one another; the purpose of worshipping together; the purpose of seeking together; the purpose of working together and the purpose of protecting one another. We are not created and made to live together for the purpose of rivalry and fierce competitions nor the purpose of surviving at the expense of the other. God made us to love one another.

What the Mind Thinks, the Man Acts

We are created in the image and likeness of God. We are endowed with intellect and will. Out of the whole creation, we are the one created with sound reason and coherent thinking. We are created with wisdom, knowledge and understanding. We are given a mind that is beyond any working machine one can think of. This machine works according to how it is configured. It is God-given brief-case of knowledge.

The human mind has been defined as a brain box that it is only God who knows what it contains. This brain box has been responsible for the character of man. It is the central unit of human behaviour. It is a treasure well protected and divinely made, given to the bearer for proper management. It is said that a man's mind may be compared with a garden, with different kinds of fruits, shrubs and flowers intelligently cultivated or allowed to grow wild and fallow. The subtle thing about the mind is that whether cultivated or not it must be growing. It brings forth good fruits when properly cultivated or wild fruits when not cultivated. This shows that the mind is a fertile ground for planting.

James Allen ascertains this when he writers:

"Just as a gardener cultivates his plot, keeping it free from weeds, and growing the flowers and fruits which he requires, so may a man tend the garden of his mind, weeding out all the wrong, useless, and impure thoughts, and cultivating toward perfection in flowers and fruits of right, useful and pure thoughts. By pursuing this process, a man sooner or later discovers that he is the master-gardener of his soul, the director of his life. He also reveals, within himself, the laws of thought, and understands with ever-increasing accuracy, how the thought-forces and mind elements operate in the shaping of his character, circumstances and destiny" (J. Maurus, 2001: 23). Jean Gutton says that the first quality of the mind is good sense. And to have good sense is to be able to discern the dividing lines between the true and the false, the just and the unjust, the excessive and the moderate by means of an insight so sudden that is functions like one of the senses(Ibid: 27).

What the mind thinks is what he reproduces as his character. If he conceives well, he reaps good character, but if the mind dwells in evil, then one should not be surprise the kind of character he exhibits. No one can tell what the mind has installed. Sometimes the faces produce contrarily what the mind plans. A friend deceives a friend because the deception is hidden in the bottom-ness of the heart. We cannot argue that many have modelled their heart in a way that there is no room for tolerance and mercy. Betrayals and sabotage are committed with bright faces and laughter; else the evil of the mind could be exposed. But no one who plans evil in his heart can achieve good at the end. From the abundance of the mind we act. Whether we like it or not, our characters spring from the foundations of the heart. Sometimes we talk, especially when angry, vomiting things that are cruel to the ear; things that one would not have said without dwelling in evil thoughts.

This is why St. Paul urges us , "Let your minds be filled with everything that is true, everything that is honourable, everything that is upright and pure, everything that we love and admire – with whatever is good and praiseworthy"(Phil 4:8). This is because he knows that the human mind, if not tendered brings evil. He also advices us, against self-indulgence which is the reason for bad temper, disagreements, factions and malice, drunkenness, antagonisms and rivalry, jealousy, envy, sexual vices, impurities and sensuality(Gal 5:18-21).

Living Together Requires Forming Our Characters

Since man is created to live together and work together for a common goal, we need to form our way of life to suit all. We cannot live like beasts, animal that live by the **survival of the fittest.** God put us together to watch each other's back. We must be our brother's keepers. We must practice virtues and detest vices. There must be a common rule of life each and every one of us must follow. These general norms, with their "Dos" and "Don'ts" form the way should behave. This is character formation.

Our characters can be given a better formation when we try to fine tune our minds. Though the late Bishop Fulton Sheen will say that character is not in the mind but in the will, we see that the weeding of the mind helps to form our intellect and will by presenting to them a fertile ground to build on. That is why it is said, "Watch your thoughts it becomes words, watch your words it becomes actions, watch your actions it becomes character, watch your characters it becomes destiny." This also tells us that we have a right to our destiny; to make it positive or negative. We make it positive when our lives and destinies yield positive result, and negative when the outcome of our lives only leave us with regrets and frustrations. And it is when regrets and frustrations set in that we grow envious of others who managed their destiny well. So to avoid that, we must work on our characters in order to shape our destiny.

CHAPTER TWO

ENVY: THE FRUIT OF AN AMBITIOUS MIND

The philosopher Aristotle, in his "Rhetoric", has defined envy as "the pain caused by the good fortune of other". while another philosopher Emmanuel Kant in his metaphysics says that envy is a "reluctance to see our own well-being overshadowed by another's because the standard we use to see how well off we are is not the intrinsic worth of our own well being but how it compares with that of others".

Generally, the term envy is best defined as a resentful emotion that occurs when a person lacks another's superior quality. It focuses on achievements or possessions of others, and either desire them or wish to acquire. It is also called invidiousness.

Envy can also be derived from a sense of low self-esteem that results from a upward social comparison threatening a person's self-image. This is a case where another person, Mr A has something that the envier Mr B. Considers being important to have. Mr B, the envier thinks that he or she should have been the one who had the desired object. Why should it be Mr A? Why shouldn't it be Mr B .In this situation Envy sets in, and it brings unhappiness and gloomy environment.

It was another philosopher, Bertrand Russell who said that envy was one of the most potent causes of unhappiness. Yes where there is envy, there bound to be feelings of insecurity, lack of peace of mind and malicious thoughts will rule over the being of the envier.

Envy is said to be a "human thing", in the sense that it is unfortunately part of human nature. This is because not only is the envious person rendered unhappy by his envy, but also wishes to inflict misfortune on others.

Psychologist, on their own part, recently, has suggested that there may be two types of envy: malicious envy and benign envy, here benign envy is proposed as a type of positive motivational force.

To classified envy can be somewhat controversial in the sense that there is no doubt that it is a negative feeling. Envy comes with the feelings of distress, rejection, detestation, that the "rival" has been an object of the target for the envier. Either that he misses the achievement or he never had the opportunity to get it .Thus instead of accepting his/her fate, his feelings focused on the one who has it. And this feeling is total rejection, not of the object but of the person who has the object.

Is Envy an Emotion?

Now the controversy is whether envy is an emotion or not. Emotion is complex psychological experience of individual's state of mind as interacting with biochemical (internal) and environmental (external) influences.

Emotion is associated with mood, temperament, personality, disposition, and motivation. Here motivations direct and energize behaviour, while emotion provides the effective components to positive or negative motivation. Thus people often behave in a certain ways as direct result of their emotional state, such as crying, fighting or fleeing. If one has the emotional without a corresponding behaviour, then we may   consider the behaviour not to be essential to the emotion

An important means of distinguishing emotion concerns their occurrence in time. Some occur over a period of seconds. For instance, "surprise" one can be surprise at a flash, whereas others can last for years, example, and love. The feelings of love do not come at a flash and can last through a person's life. The feeling of love could be regarding as a certain object rather than emotions proper. There is also what is called "emotion episodes and dispositions.

Emotion dispositions are also comparable to character traits, where someone may be said to be generally disposed to experience certain emotions, though about different object. For instance an irritable person is generally disposed to feel irritation more easily or quickly than others do.

Some theorists like Klaus Scherer places emotions within a more general category of "affective state" where affective state can also include emotion related phenomena such as pleasure and pain, and motivational state like hunger and curiosity, moods dispositions and traits.

Thus strictly speaking envy cannot be regarded as an emotion, however, there is a wide spread assumption that it is indeed an emotion as well as a mere feeling.

"Envy   occurs when someone begrudges another

Individual for his or her possessions or attributes,

Or when an individual longs for the others

Possessions and attribute

CHAPTER THREE

JEALOUSY: THE BURNING FIRE THAT LEADS TO DESTRUCTION

Oftentimes envy and jealousy are confused and used interchangeable, which is inappropriate. While the target of envy or the cause of envy is other's possession, jealousy involves people, for instance, Mr. Jonathan buys a brand new pathfinder jeep. And Dr. Chris, his colleague and friends lust over the new car and wished that he (Dr. Chris) could buy a brand new pathfinder jeep as well, there is an envy on the object – jeep .though Dr. Chris state of mind could be involved his psychological states such as utility, happiness, or superiority could play an effective part in his next time of action. This is envy.

On the other hand, jealousy is a secondary emotion and typically refers to the negative thoughts and feelings of insecurity, fear and anxiety over an anticipated loss of something that the person valves, particularly in reference to human connection. Jealousy often consists of a combination of presenting emotions such as anger, sadness, resentment and disgust. It is not to be confused with envy.

Jealousy is often reinforce as a series of particularly

strong emotions and constructed as a universal human experience; it has been a theme of many artistic works that seek to privilege monogamous discourses .but different field demonstrate it in different ways.

1. Psychologists: This has proposed several models of the processes underlying jealousy and has identified factors that result in jealousy. we will see these later.
2. Sociologists: These have demonstrated that cultural beliefs and valves play an important role in determining what triggers jealousy and what constitute socially acceptable expression of jealousy.
3. Biologists: these have identified factors that may unconsciously influence the expression of jealousy .Artists have explored the theme of jealousy in photographs, paintings, movies, songs, plays, poems, and book.

   There is also theological perspective of jealousy which has to do with religious views based on the scriptures of different faiths.

a) ENVY AND JEALOUSY IN RELATIONSHIP

We need to talk about these negative emotions in human relationship because they lead to rivalry, conflicts and disintegration of already built relationship. First of all, let us look at genders in the relationship, whether male to female, or male to male or female to female relationship. Let us first discuss this on gender difference.

b) GENDER DIFFERENCES

According to the parental investment model based on parental investment theory, more men than women ratify sex difference in jealousy. In addition, more women over men consider emotional infidelity or, fear of abandonment, as more distressing than sexual infidelity. According to researcher, sex and attachment style makes significant and unique interactive contributions to the distress experienced. Security within the relationship also heavily contributes to one's distress level. Also according to researchers, these finding imply that psychological and cultural mechanism regarded sex differences may play a larger role than expected.

According to Schachner and Shaer, (2004:67), individuals with dismissing behaviour were more concerned with the sexual aspect of relationships. As a coping mechanism these individuals would report sexual infidelity as more harmful. Moreover research shows that audit attachment styles strongly conclude with the type of infidelity that occurred. Thus psychological and cultural mechanism is implied as unvarying differences in jealousy that play a role in sexual attachment.

Emotional jealousy was predicted to be nine times more responsive in females than in males. The emotional jealousy predicted in females also held turn to state that females experiencing emotional jealousy are more violent than men experiencing emotional jealousy.

Buss, Green and Saboni give distinct emotional responses to gender differences in romantic relationships. For example, due to paternity uncertainty in males, jealousy increases in males over sexual infidelity rather than emotional. According to their research more women are likely to be upset by signs of resource withdraw than by sexual infidelity. A large amount of data supports this notion. However, one must consider for jealousy the life stage or experience one encounter in reference to the diverse responses to infidelity available. Research states that a componential view of jealously consists of specific set of emotions that serve the reproductive role. However it shows that both men and women would be equally angry and point the blame for sexual infidelity, but women would be more hurt by emotional infidelity. Despite this fact, angry surfaces when both parties involved is responsible for some type of uncontrollable characters. However hurt feelings are activated by relationship deviation.

c) ROMANTIC JEALOUSY

Romantic jealousy can be experienced in long-term or

short-term relationships. One partner can feel the emotion of jealousy arise if the other partner is paying more attention or time to someone else. To lose services from one partner and have their attention directed towards someone else does not have to be in romantic way. One partner could be spending more time with a friend that no romantic feelings could ever develop.

d) FRIENDSHIP OR PLATONIC JEALOUSY

Jerry was so fond of his friend Juan. They were so close that people thought them to be inseparable. But this relationship has been built on Jerry's undying love. He loved Juan so much that he pets her, cares for her and tried to give his best in seeing that Juan was okay. Juan was not reciprocating this honest love. She was not always there for him. She was not as caring as Jerry was. But Jerry was not minding. All he knew was that he loved her. So everything was going on well until Jerry met Julia, a very humble and kind-hearted nurse who helped him and took good care of him while he was admitted in the hospital. Jerry was taken to the kind heart of Julia and started enjoying her company and love. Juan was furious and could not bear seeing another lady coming to take her man away from her. She used a strategy – pretence. She pretended to love Julia's help and friendly gestures but was planning to eliminate her. She hired three men who went to Julia's residence and bathed her with an acid. This is a form of Jealousy referred to as Friendship or Platonic Jealousy.

This is a form of jealousy that is seen in friendships. Platonic jealousy is similar to romantic jealousy in the way that this type of relationship can lead to jealousy in result of fear of being replaced, having competition or being compared to a third party. For instance, the intense emotion of jealousy can arise if two friends that are females decide that they like the same man and both want to start a romantic relationship with him. Comparison and competition will more often than not lead to the two females experiencing the emotion of jealousy. This could bring about fierce rivalry and even killing of any of the females, as the struggles continues.

e) SIBLING RIVALRY

The biblical Joseph and his brothers clearly points to the sibling jealousy or rivalry. Joseph was the second to the last child of Jacob. He was so much loved and cherished by his father that much attention was given to him more than any of his sibling. He was honest and humble. He brings good feedback and reports to his father. Joseph reports even the evil deeds of some of his brothers to the father. This made him to be loved by the father and hated by his brothers. This hatred grew so fierce that the brothers started planning to kill him. They were hiding their evil thoughts as they pretended to love him. When they went to take care of their father's flock, they wasted so much time that Jacob, their father sent Joseph to go and look for them. As Joseph was approaching, they strategize their plans to eliminate him. Joseph's brothers sold him into slavery, not knowing that they were selling him into the fulfilment of his destiny. This is sibling jealousy or rivalry.

Sibling rivalry is a common form of family jealousy. Family jealousy can affect all ages and different members of any family. This jealousy can arise from lack of attention from a specific member in the family. More attention toward another member of the family can cause this emotion or the emotion can be seen through comparison to another member in the family. This type of jealousy is once again in result of losing some sort of attention or services that someone once had, or that they believe that they had.

Jacob has not shared his attention to all his children, this we may think, but Joseph was favoured because he was a child after the father's heart. He does what the father wants and was given a reward of special attention. In our families, this kind of incident could be the case. Sometimes attentions are not given equally but this should not spring jealousy and rivalry since we have the same purpose and the same goal.

The family be a place where, no matter who is loved most, all should work for the same goal. The love and care of the family, anyways, should not be unjustly apportioned to few while neglecting others so as to avoid arousing the feeling of jealousy. Parents and guidance should love their children equally, though some may be favoured more than others because of their efforts and characters. Sibling rivalry should not be seen in the family, when this happens, it can grow into enmity between brothers and sisters

f) WORK PLACE JEALOUSY

One of my Parishioners came to me the other day begging for prayers and counselling. I asked him what his problem was all about, and he was shivering as he told me the story of his friend who was poisoned because he was promoted at their working place. Mr. Martin (the victim), was promoted to the office of the General Manager of their company. One of the senior staff, Mr. Kenneth, his bosom friend, was not happy because he thought the position would have gone his way. He could not contend a junior to him being promoted ahead of him. He was envious and planned to eliminate him. Mr. Kenneth pretended to appreciate the new G.M, and was singing his praises. He even went to the extent of popping wine for him to show his solidarity and support for the new General Manager. Later that same week, Mr. Kenneth took Mr. Martin to a restaurant to celebrate the promotion.

Unknowing to Martin, Kenneth has allied with the restaurant attendant and poisoned his food. Now the post was vacant and Gilbert, my young parishioner was giving the post to occupy as the interim General Manager. Given to the circumstance of the position, Gilbert was so scared that he now feared his dear life because no one is to be trusted. This is a kind of Jealousy called "Work Place" Jealousy.

Jealousy in the work place or market place is not uncommon. People can experience another in practically any setting that one person feels like they are losing services from something or someone else. This type of jealousy is often seen between colleagues in similar job positions. If one worker receives positive feedback from the boss while the other employee feels like they deserve that, positive feedback jealousy can arise. Jealousy between colleagues can also arise if the employees are working for a raise or trying to undo each other for similar job positions. Once again, the attention received towards one employee and not the other may cause intense emotions of jealousy to develop.

CHAPTER FOUR

POWER AND INFLUENCE: HOW WE CAN GET TO THE TOP

In the Shakespearean work, Macbeth, we saw how power can drive one to kill. Power and the love to acquire it can make a friend betray his friend, a father kill his son, and a son destroy his own father. Macbeth killed his Cousin King Duncan in other to attain the position of a King. Today's polities bear many Macbeths who are ready to murder in other to achieve their ambition. Power-drive is quite dangerous.

The reign of Libyan dictator Muammar Qaddafi came to an end last week at the hand of a combination of rebel and UN forces. Qaddafi – at least according to the American news media and some of his own people - was widely considered a tyrannical ruler who stifled free expression and democracy during his 40years of rule. Whenever I think of men like Qaddafi, something tells me that a situation has created tyrant we now know that there is something about power that changes people, and transform them to ruthless and oppressive individuals.

There are three things that should be taken into cognizance here: The first being that power corrupts; that absolute power corrupts absolutely. Basically, we have the anecdotes that support this Myth well in hand: countless Governors, Presidents, and senators have engaged in immoral and unlawful actions, and it is easy to believe, base on this evidences, that power is a special corrupting force that renders even the most saintly of men into sinners.

1 POWER DOESN'T CORRUPT EVERYONE

In some cases, the thought that power corrupts could be untrue given that not all leaders are corrupt. For instance, in 2001, professor Serena Chen and her colleagues examined how selfish or selfless individuals would behave when put in a position of power. Chen and colleagues gave participants in their experiment control over resources and punishment of another individual and then measured aspects of their personality. The personality measure assessed the extent to which the participant tended to be communal – a selfless sharer of goods, favours, and resources or exchange oriented - selfish calculi what one is owed by others. Participants were there given an opportunity to help another participant during the experiment. The result was definitive: selfish power holders were selfish during the experiment, and they failed to help their partners. Selfless power holders, on the other hand, actually continued to be selfless and helpful even when they were give power. The moral of this story is that power doesn't corrupt everyone. Only the greed is intoxicated with power, and they want to acquire everything. It is this kind of people who kill, eliminate and back-bite others to acquire power. The greedy people use many tools to achieve their goals: blackmails, political propaganda, assassination and other evil manipulations to acquire power.

2 FIX YOURSELF IN THE CORRIDORS OF POWER

A lot of stories about power suggest that there is only one kind of power, and you either have it or you don't. When we think about our coaches in sports, political leaders, and managers we often think of examples of individuals who are large in physical size, most often male, respected and admired by their peer, and who make most of the decisions. For instance, Abraham Lincoln – the prototype for a US president – was tall; male respected, and made decisions. It's easy, base on this thought processes, to think there is only one type of power or status.

But statistics, however, suggest that there are different types of power and status. For instance, physical dominance may mean you are a man with high levels of testosterone, but this might not help you make decisions in the board room where physical stature has less influence. Similarly, if we look harder at our politicians we might remember that many of these individuals have power to make decisions even when they are not respected or admired. The current American president, Barrack Obama is rated high in this aspect.

A person may have decision – making power even when they come from families that are low in socioeconomic status. Research is beginning to suggest that power and status are much more context- specific than we realized. One must fix himself or herself appropriately on the condors' of power .You have some endowed qualities that suit a different character of power which the other person lacks. Eliminating the other because of his/her qualities cannot be the solution. The proper solution is to work on your qualities that suit that particular power you desire that particular position's one may be good in decision making, the other good in restructuring ideas and the other still in executing ideas. What corrupts absolutely is absolute power.

3 YOU DON'T HAVE TO BREAK THE RULES

Some people believe you must belong to a cult, lie, cheat, kill and steal your way to the top. But is that true? Think for a moment about a time that you might have been passed over for promotion in favour of one of your rivals .why do you think you were passed over? Probably because the other person was scheming their way to the top by breaking at least 2-3 laws and 3-4 of your moral rules. The reality is that getting to the top of a social hierarchy is a little less sinister then this. It's less about being unethical and more about appearing competent.

The psychologist, Michael Kraus, gives two lines of research that suggest that appearing competent matters for status attainment. In the first aspect,

People are nominated to leadership when they appear to be competent. That is , independent of their actual ability to solve problems ,if a person simply appear to know how to solve problems, in social group ,settings (by offering suggestions and expressing ideas) he/she will be nominated to a leadership position.

All these should give us hope, more than anything else, about the leaders of tomorrow. It turns out that leaders are not universally corruptible, that power in one setting doesn't mean power in another, and that you are not being passed over at work by immoral jerks- at least not exclusively. You don't have to enter a secret cult to acquire power nor do you have to kill and blackmail and break rules to be nominated to a position in the society. You only have to work on your character and abilities. You have to prove yourself competent enough to be selected.

CHAPTER FIVE

GREED AND MATERIALISM

Greed and materialism stand in opposition to any manifestation of true happiness. This is another drive that makes people betray their bosom friends and even deny their parents. Greed and materialism has turned many saints to sinners and made some Christians go diabolical. The love of wealth and material things have made so many people sell their souls. People are under a false perception that money will solve all of their problems and as a result brings them their utmost joy and happiness. This is why many are avaricious and greed in seeking material wealth. Greed has fierce consequences and can lead to envy and stealing. It is a common phenomenon in our world today. Greed is commonly seen in a working place, politics, economic environments, and even in our families. It is the peak of the pack.

The word 'Greed' is an excessive desire to possess wealth, goods or abstract things of value with the intention to keep it for oneself. Greed is inappropriate expectations. It involves a very excessive or rapacious desire and pursuit of wealth, status and power. The word, Greed is used to criticize those who seek excessive material wealth, although it may apply to the need to feel more excessively moral, social or otherwise better than someone else.

According to St. Thomas Aquinas, "Greed was a sin against God, just as all mortal sins, inasmuch as man condemns things eternal for the seek of temporal things." Meher Barba dictated that, "Greed is a state of restlessness of the heart, and it consist mainly of craving for power and possessions. Possession and power is sort for the fulfilment of desires."

Materialism, on the other hand, is such a worldwide problem today that many authors use, this as a theme and a character trait in their literary work. Materialism is mindset that uses the consumption and acquisition of material goods as positive and desirable. It is often bound up with a value system which regards social status as being intrinsically linked to affluence as well as the perception that happiness can be increased through buying, spending and accumulating material wealth.

Guy de Maupassant represents in "The Necklace," his central character Madame Moisel as a poor, greed, envious woman, who wants nothing more in life than material wealth. In the book , "if you touched my Heart" by Isabelle Allende , you see Amadeo , the protagonist who has all the money that he needs and still he chooses to corrupt a young woman's life for his own sick desires.

In our societies today, many are greedy, and it shows in their relationship with others. They are not satisfied with what they have, they want to acquire more. This also could be seen among the youths – male and female. They want to acquire the best in the series. They have unbridled quest for the latest materials in town. We cannot invent but are curiously searching for the latest inventions. Materialism has cause conflicts between friends, and many have lost their lives as consequence of their lust for material things.

Greedy and materialistic people rejoice in others' misfortune because they expect some material or emotional gain. That is why Gore Vidal will say, "It is not enough to succeed; others must fail". Greed and materialism begets malice, and malice is like a game of poker or tennis; you don't play it with anyone who is manifestly inferior to you.

a) **THE EMOTION OF "PLEASURE-IN- OTHERS' – MISFORTUNE"**

For greed and materialism people, it normal to be pleased with other's misfortune and be displeased with others success. But it would appear morally more perverse to be pleased with another's person's misfortune than too be displeased with another person's good fortune. Indeed the philosophers Arthur

Schopenhauer, argues that "to feel envy is human, but to enjoy other people misfortune is diabolical". Foe Schopenhauer, pleasure-in-others'-misfortune is the worst trait in human nature since it is closely related to cruelty.

In describing pleasure-in-others'-misfortune. These features describe a significant conflict between our positive evaluation of the situation and the negative evaluation of the other person. This conflict indicates the presence of a comparative, and sometimes even, a competitive, concern. A major reason for being pleased with the misfortune of another person is that this person's misfortune may somehow benefit us; it may, for example, emphasize our superiority.

WHY SOME LIKE TO SEE OTHERS CRY

It is not sufficient to characterize pleasure-in-others'-misfortune as including our pleasure and the other's misfortune. I would like to suggest three additional typical characteristics:

1. The other person is perceived to deserve the misfortune.
2. The misfortune is relatively minor.
3. We are passive in generating the other's misfortune.

Deserved misfortune: here a central feature of pleasure-in-others'-misfortune is the belief that the other person deserves her misfortune. For instance, when stuck in a traffic jam, should a driver pass us, on our right by driving on the hard shoulders, our anger will be replaced with pleasure when we see a policeman giving the driver a severe punishment for wrong driving. The belief that the other person deserves his misfortune expresses our assumption that justice has been done and enables us to be pleased in a situation where we seem required to be sad.

Moreover, this belief presents us as moral people who do not want to hurt other people. The more deserved the misfortune is, the more justified is the pleasure. Norman Feathers shows in a study of people's attitudes towards the down-fall of those in high positions that the fall was greeted positive approval when the fall was seen to be deserved, but reactions were negative when the fall was seen to be undeserved. But whether deserved or not, the cries of other people should not bring pleasure. People do make mistakes which can lead to their fall; it should not cause us pleasure. It is only when there is greed, hatred and envy that the fall of others, whether deserved or not, is pleasurable.

When misfortune is minor: the second characteristics of pleasure-in-others'-misfortune concerns the minor nature of the misfortune. This characteristic is associated with comparative concern prevailing in this emotion. Comparison is possible when the two parties are not too far apart, when they are considered to belong to the same comparative framework. Accordingly liking-to-see-others- often turns into pity. For instance, should our noisy in considerate and snobbish neighbour find out that his wife is having an affair, we may feel some pleasure; however, if his daughter becomes seriously ill, we are more likely to feel compassion or pity. We can admit that in some circumstances the other's misfortune may be grave, but it is still not significantly graver than that cause by this person to the other people – especially ourselves and those related to us. Some will be pleased when Qadaffi was murdered or when Osama Bin Laden was killed just because such a murderer seems "well deserved" given to what they did to innocent people.

When associated with passivity: pleasure-in-others'-misfortune is associated with the passivity of the agent enjoying the situation. An active personal involvement is contrary to the rules of fair competition; it would present us as deliberately harming the other, and hence as not being the real winner in the ongoing competition. It may also be considered as offense; although the other person might deserve misfortune, or even punishment, we lack the authority, as human beings, to impose it.

Some people identify pleasure-in-others'-misfortune with sadism, arguing that the difference between them is negligible and pleasure-in-others'-misfortune often has a public image, but this merely represents extreme cases. Also there would seem little in common between romantic love, which involves a positive attitude towards the beloved, and the negative attitude of pleasure-in-others'-misfortune. However, it can be present when the misfortune is very minor and the partner responds to the misfortune humorously or by teasing a response that is part of a loving relationship, as are other type of games.

It is, however, more common in loving relationships when a third party is involved, or when the romantic relationship failed. Considering the following case described a student: "Last winter, i had a lover, who had this awful girl friend. Some days after i had an aching throat, I heard them talking on the phone, and she did not feel well and that her throat ached. Well, the smile on my face was not easy to conceal." In another case, Loveth is joyful over the infidelity of Mary's husband Samuel, since Mary used to be her own husband's lover. Mar y may suffer a great deal because of Samuel's infidelity, and Loveth may know it, nevertheless, in enjoying this event, Loveth thinks that justice has been done and that Mary's suffering resembles her own, thus putting them on equal footing. In some cases the others' misfortune may be substantial, but is not much greater than what used to be, or still be our own misfortune. But is this justice?

Sometimes the profound pain of losing a lover may generate pathological attitude which is even worse than pleasure-in-others'-misfortune. A real example like this is that of a man whose wife had an affair, and as a result they divorced. The wife married her lover and shortly afterwards, gave birth to a son. A few years later when the child developed cancer, the man expressed pleasure that his ex-wife has been punished. This is a pathological case since not only is the wife's misfortune far too severe but misfortune is shared by an innocent child. Evil cannot be used to avenge evil. Also any evil that causes pleasure points to the fact that there is no love. Love surpasses all wrong.

CONCLUSION

Thomas Jefferson regretting on man's inhumanity to man says, "What a stupendous, what an incomprehensible machine is man! Who can endure toil, famine, stripes, imprisonment and death itself in vindication of his own liberty, and the next moment, inflict on his fellow men a bondage, one hour of which is fraught with more misery than ages of that which he rose in rebellion to oppose." And James Carroll affirms that we cloak ourselves in cold indifference to the unnecessary suffering of others...even when we cause it. Human beings sometimes walk around with a meaningless life. They seem half-asleep, even when they are busy doing things they think important. This is because some people chase the wrong things or the right things in a wrong way or through wrong means. But we tend to ignore the fact that the way one gets meaning into his or her life is to devote oneself to loving others, devote oneself to his or her community around you, and devote oneself to creating something that gives him or her purpose and meaning in life. We lack our purpose when focus on individuals instead of ideas. That is when envy, jealousy, blackmailing and backbiting come into one's life.

I want to conclude this work by saying that we have

the opportunity to revise the hand the clock insofar as we are still alive. We should not be crying over spilled Champagne. Amend must be made the way we relate with people. But we must begin the sanitary work from our own selves. We must weed our minds of jealousy and envy. Let us learn the way of success instead of fighting those who have succeeded. We must be careful or unfaithful friends and be wary of faithful enemies. Nobody has enough and no one can get enough. The best is to be content with what we have. Though we can have ambition but over ambition is a crime. It exposes one to evil thoughts. There is something perverse about more than enough. When we have more, it is never enough. It is always somewhere out there, just out of reach. The more we acquire, the more elusive enough becomes. Let us work on our virtues and build our lives on them, whatever will be ours must surely come our way.

REFERENCES

1. J. MAURUS – "Use Your Stress: To Keep away Distress", Better yourself Books, Bombay, 2005.
2. J. MAURUS – "A Source Book of inspiration: Quotations, Anecdotes, Humour, Mumbai, 2001.
3. Robert Greene: "48 Laws of Power", first South Asian Edition, 2003.
4. Robert H. Schuller: "You Can Become the Person You Want To Be", A jove Book, 1973.
5. Shaun Harry, "Today's Psychology: the dimension of the self", Harry and Bruce Books, Manchester, 2004.